POODLES

FAVORITE DOG BREEDS

Dan Lopez

Norwood House Press

Cataloging-in-Publication Data

Names: Lopez, Dan.
Title: Poodles / Dan Lopez.
Description: Buffalo, NY : Norwood House Press, 2027. | Series: Favorite dog breeds | Includes glossary and index.
Identifiers: ISBN 9781978580381 (pbk.) | ISBN 9781978580398 (library bound) | ISBN 9781978580404 (ebook)
Subjects: LCSH: Poodles--Juvenile literature. | Dog breeds--Juvenile literature.
Classification: LCC SF429.P85 L67 2027 | DDC 636.728--dc23

Published in 2027 by
Norwood House Press
2544 Clinton Street
Buffalo, NY 14224

Designer: Rhea Magaro
Editor: Tricia Hoffman

Photo credits: Cover, p.1 Anna Averianova/Shutterstock.com; p.5 Tymoshenko Olga/Shutterstock.com; p.6 Linas T/Shutterstock.com; p.7 everydoghasastory/Shutterstock.com; p.8 De Jongh Photography/Shutterstock.com; p.9 chrisukphoto/Shutterstock.com; p.10 Danita Delimont/Shutterstock.com; p.11 Mary Swift/Shutterstock.com; p.11 chrisukphoto/Shutterstock.com; p.12 Nitik/Shutterstock.com; p.14 art4you1/Shutterstock.com; p.15 New Africa/Shutterstock.com; p.17 Raywoo/Shutterstock.com; p.18 anetapics/Shutterstock.com; p.19 Teemu Tretjakov/Shutterstock.com; p.21 Lucky Business/Shutterstock.com;

Printed in the United States of America

CPSIA compliance information: Batch #CSNHP27: For further information contact Norwood House Press at 1-800-237-9932.

TABLE OF CONTENTS

Meet the Poodle

Poodles are popular pets. Dogs of this **breed** are known for having thick, curly hair that can be cut into different styles.

The poodle is the national dog of France.

toy poodle

What Do Poodles Look Like?

Poodles come in three sizes. There are toy, miniature, and standard poodles.

Toy poodles are the smallest. They stand 10 inches (25 centimeters) tall or less. They weigh six to nine pounds (three to four kilograms).

A standard poodle is the biggest. It stands up to 27 inches (69 centimeters) tall. Adults can weigh up to 70 pounds (32 kilograms)!

standard poodle

A poodle's **coat** can be white, gray, black, brown, or multi-colored. Poodles have woolly **undercoats** and wiry topcoats.

These dogs have long ears and straight **snouts**.

In the past 30 years, people have crossed poodles with other dogs to make new breeds. They chose poodles because their fur does not bother people who have **allergies**.

The Labradoodle is a mix of poodle and Labrador retriever.

Golden retrievers and poodles were bred to make goldendoodles.

A cockapoo is a cross between a cocker spaniel and a poodle.

Where Do Poodles Come From?

Poodles are popular in France, but they were first raised in Germany. Hunters trained them to fetch ducks from the water. *Poodle* comes from the German word *pudel*. It means "to splash in water."

Once, poodles were the favorite pets of kings and queens.

With their sharp sense of smell, poodles were used to hunt for **truffles**.

Do Poodles Make Good Pets?

Poodles make excellent **companions**. They are very **intelligent**. They quickly learn new things.

Poodles are strong and **athletic**. They are always ready to run and play.

These dogs love to fetch toys.

They love to swim!

What Do Poodles Need?

Poodles are **energetic**. They need exercise every day.

Their curly coats need special care. A poodle's hair should be trimmed often and brushed daily.

Glossary

allergies (AL-ur-jeez): conditions that make some people sneeze, get a rash, or have other reactions when they are exposed to certain things such as pet hair

athletic (ath-LET-ik): good at running, jumping, and other physical activities

breed (breed): one type or kind of an animal

coat (koht): the hair or fur that covers an animal's body

companions (kuhm-PAN-yuhnz): friends, buddies, or partners

energetic (en-ur-JET-ik): strong, active, and full of energy

intelligent (in-TEL-i-juhnt): quick to learn and understand; smart

snouts (snouts): the long front parts of animals' heads that include the nose and mouth

truffles (TRUH-fuls): fungi that are similar to mushrooms, that grow underground, and that are highly prized for their flavor

undercoats (UHN-dur-kohts): layers of short, soft hair that are underneath an animal's longer outer coat and that provide extra warmth

Thinking Questions

1. What are the three sizes of poodles?
2. Describe a poodle's coat.
3. What is a goldendoodle?
4. Where were poodles first bred?
5. Why do poodles make good pets for people with allergies?

Index

About the Author

Dan Lopez is a writer who loves dogs! He has a German shepherd named Hans and an Irish setter named Tam. They love to go for walks in the woods together. Sometimes, they jump in the lake for a swim. Dan lives in Indiana with his wife and three kids.